Half Position

for the Cello

by Cassia Harvey

CHP158

©2011 by C. Harvey Publications All Rights Reserved.

www.charveypublications.com - print books
www.learnstrings.com - PDF downloadable books
www.harveystringarrangements.com - chamber music

Half Position for the Cello

1

Cassia Harvey

Baltic Fiddler

©2011 C. Harvey Publications All Rights Reserved.

2

Cossack Bassist

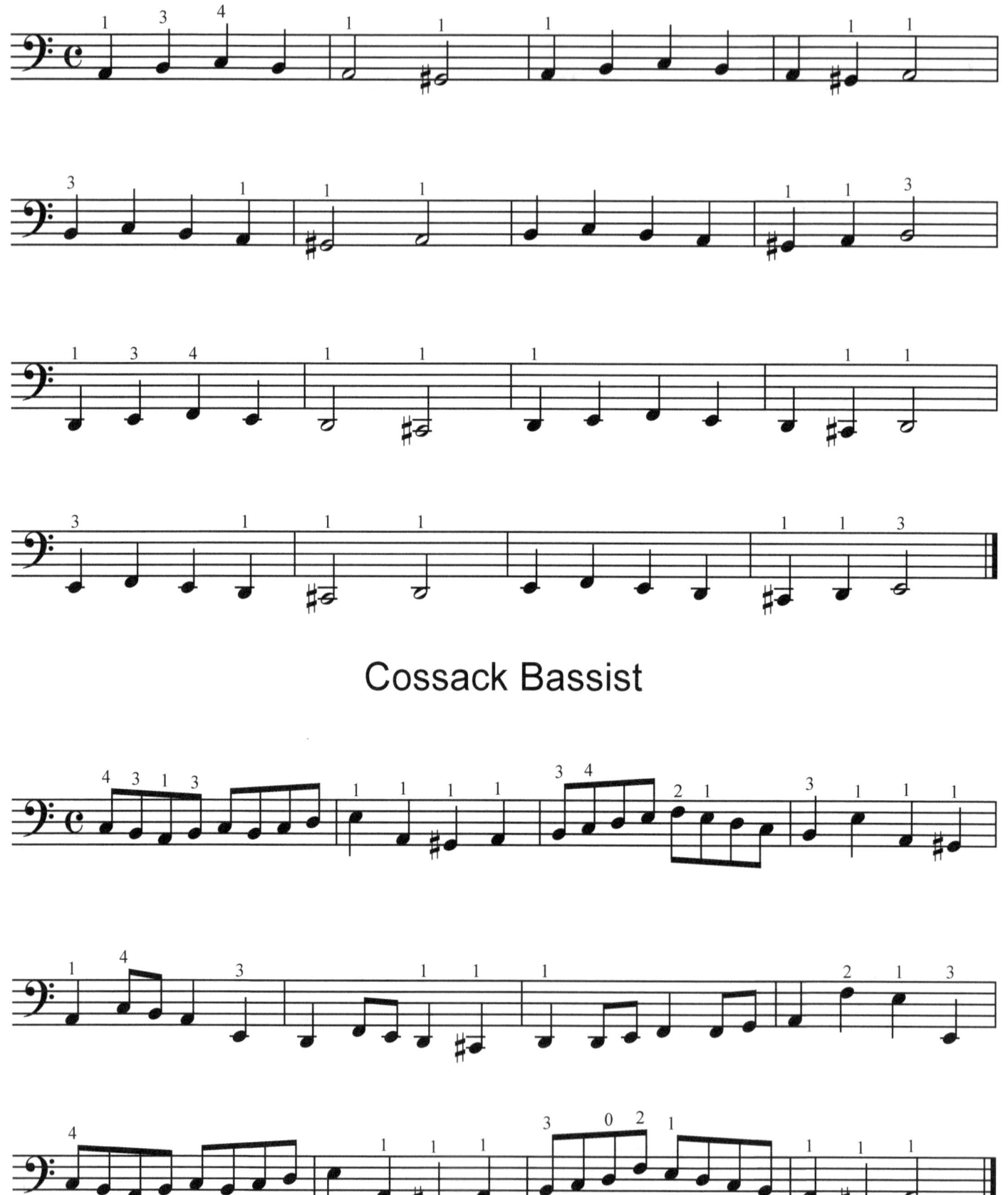

©2011 C. Harvey Publications All Rights Reserved.

4

Siberian Vista

©2011 C. Harvey Publications All Rights Reserved.

5

The Muscovite

©2011 C. Harvey Publications All Rights Reserved.

7

Half Position for the Cello

This exercise is played entirely in half position.

Perplexing Chess

Stay in half position.

©2011 C. Harvey Publications All Rights Reserved.

8

This exercise is played entirely in half position.

Chamomile Chaos

9

The Runestone

10

Caravanserai

11

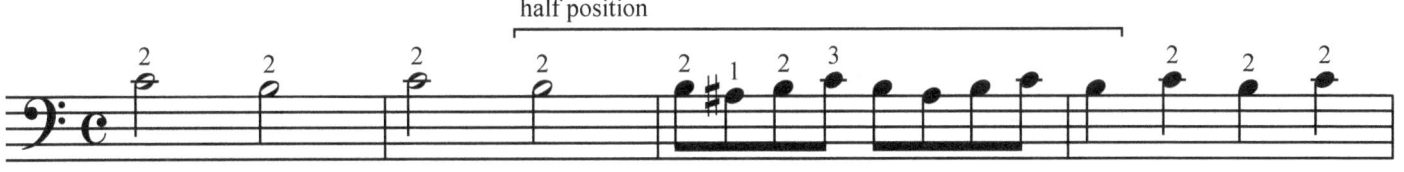

Lubec Sea Glass

12

Stay in half position.

Tendu

13

Traveling Abroad

14

Russian Folk Song

Half Position for the Cello

15

The Wind: A Russian Folk Song

©2011 C. Harvey Publications All Rights Reserved.

16

The Polar Easterlies

17

Acanthus

Half Position for the Cello

19

The Wedding: A Russian Folk Song

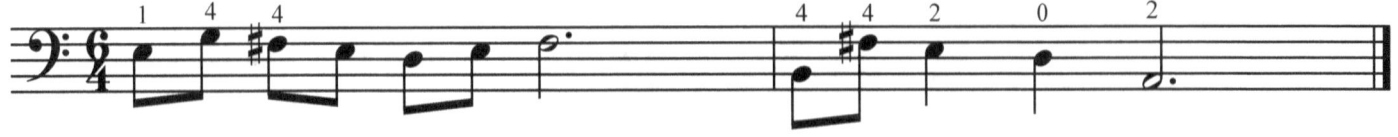

©2011 C. Harvey Publications All Rights Reserved.

20

This exercise is played entirely in half position.

Zoanthids

This piece is played entirely in half position.

Half Position for the Cello

21

This exercise is played entirely in half position.

Barn Dance

©2011 C. Harvey Publications All Rights Reserved.

22

Cerulean Blue

This piece is played entirely in half position.

Half Position for the Cello

23

This exercise is played entirely in half position.

The Catalyst

This piece is played entirely in half position.

©2011 C. Harvey Publications All Rights Reserved.

24

Stay in half position.   *Stay in half position.*

Frozen Tundra

This piece is played entirely in half position.

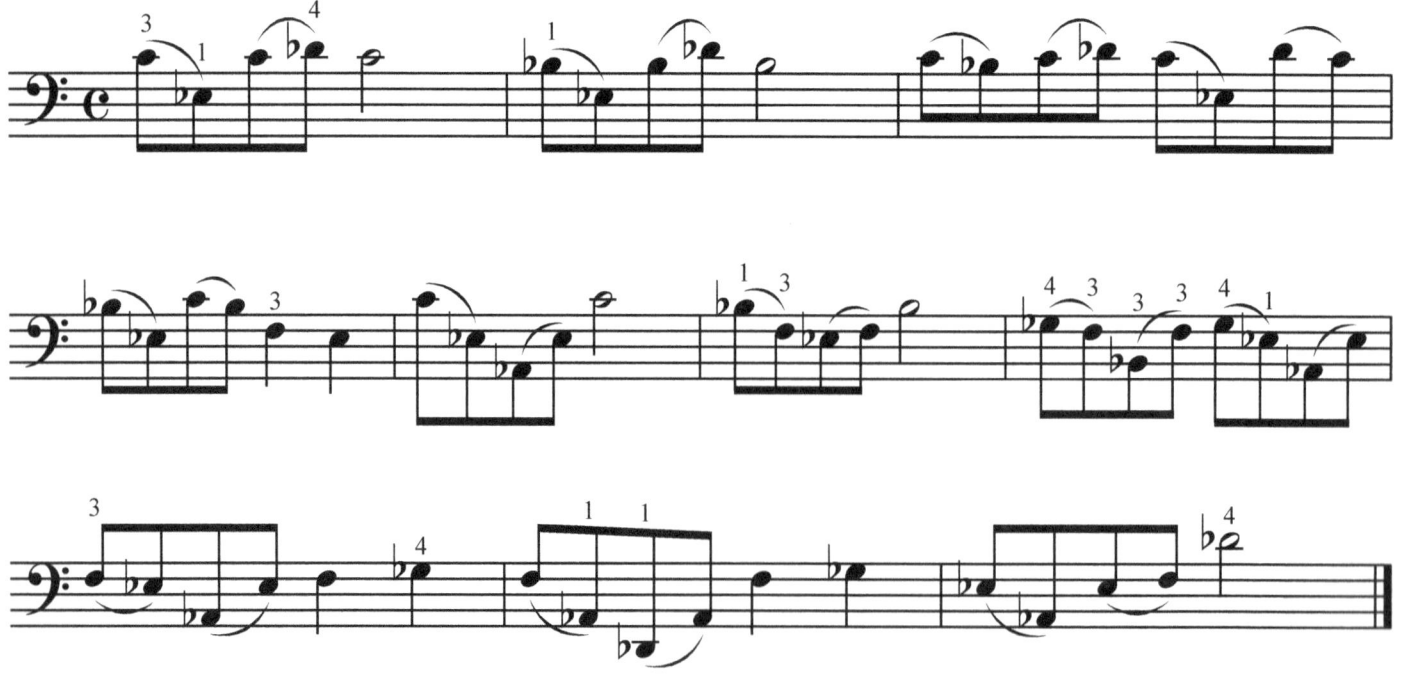

©2011 C. Harvey Publications All Rights Reserved.

Half Position for the Cello

25

Outdoors: A Russian Folk Song

©2011 C. Harvey Publications All Rights Reserved.

26

This exercise is played entirely in half position.

On the River

This piece is played entirely in half position.

Half Position for the Cello

27

Melancholy

This piece is played entirely in half position.

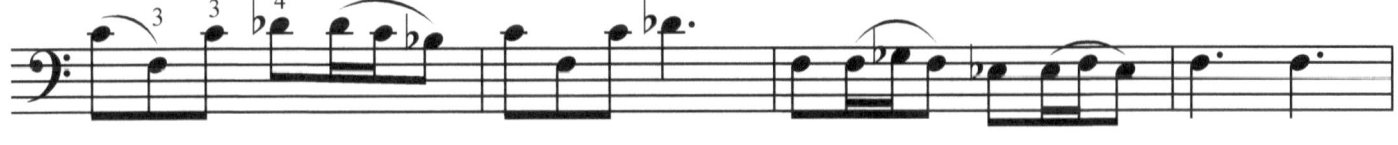

28

Stay in half position.

Purple Palette

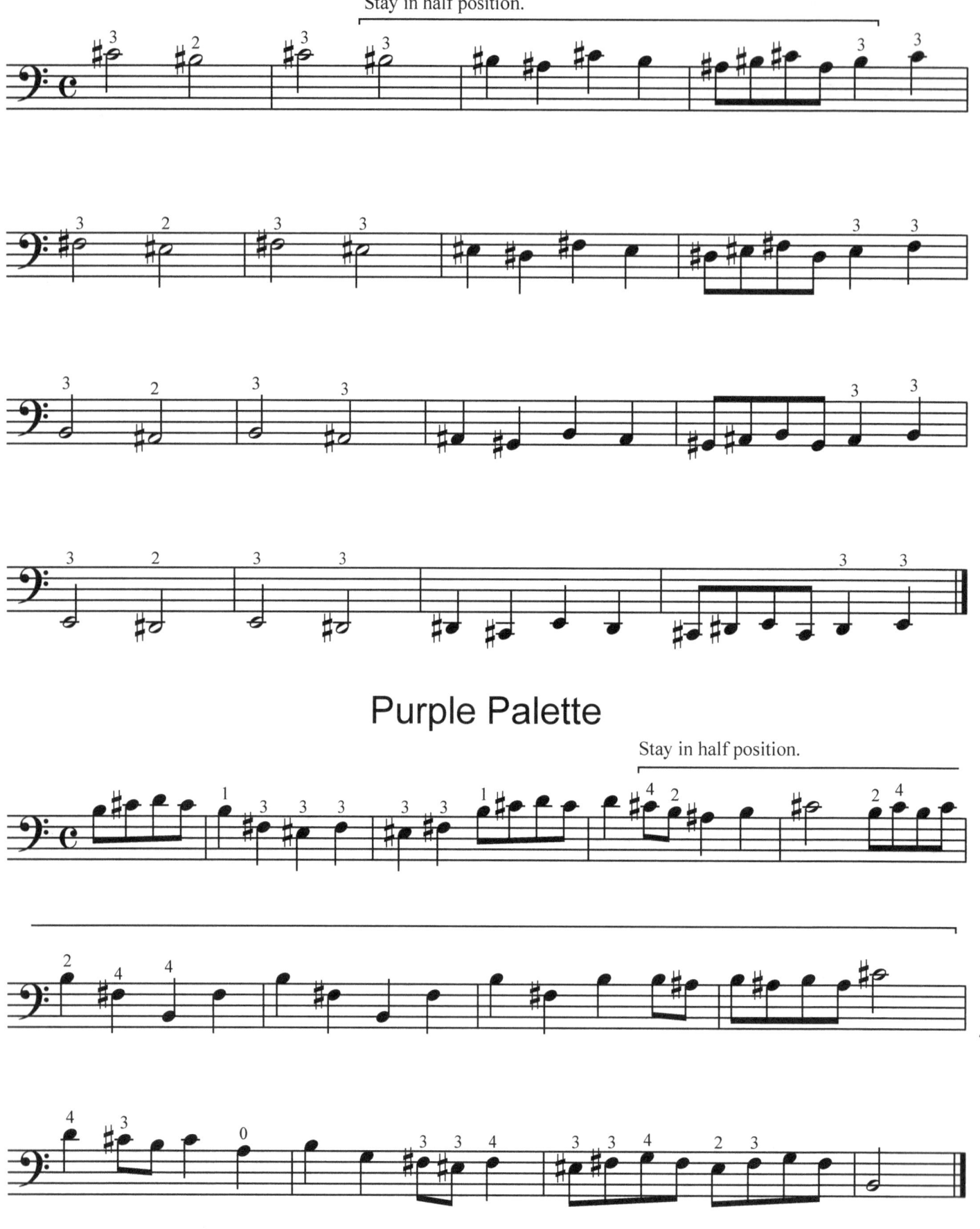

29

This exercise is played entirely in half position.

Whimsy

30

This exercise is played entirely in half position.

March

Half Position for the Cello

31

Crazy Drizzle

This piece is played entirely in half position.

©2011 C. Harvey Publications All Rights Reserved.

32

This exercise is played entirely in half position.

Rebellious Rain

This piece is played entirely in half position.

Half Position for the Cello

33

This exercise is played entirely in half position.

Russian Folk Song

Stay in half position.

©2011 C. Harvey Publications All Rights Reserved.

34

Schmoll: Song of the Cavalier

36

Boccherini: Menuet

37

Mozart: Aria from *Don Juan*

38

Sailor's Hornpipe

39

My Sweetheart: A Finnish Folk Song

40

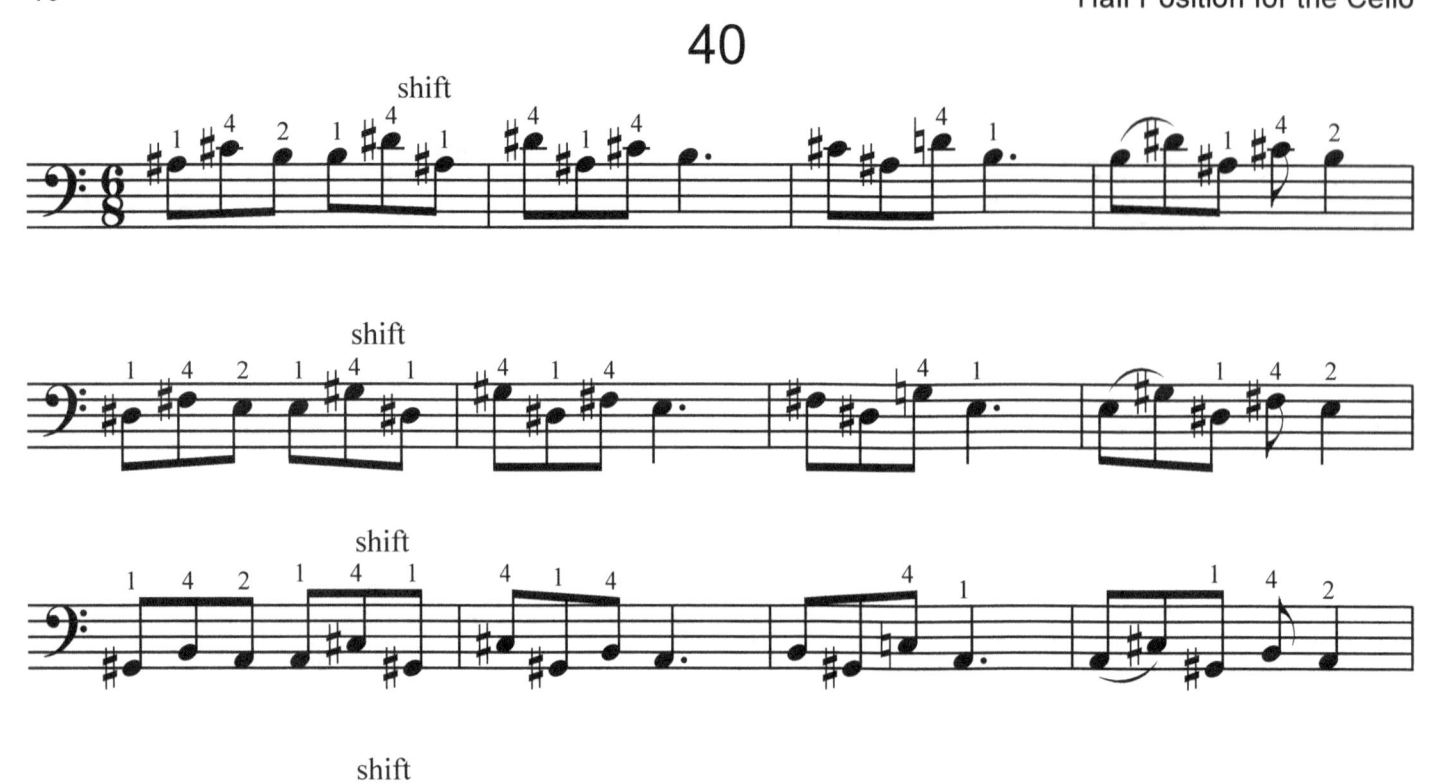

The Golden Cuckoo: A Finnish Folksong

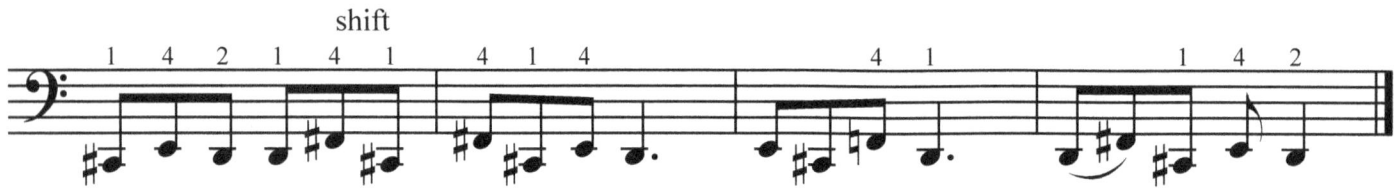

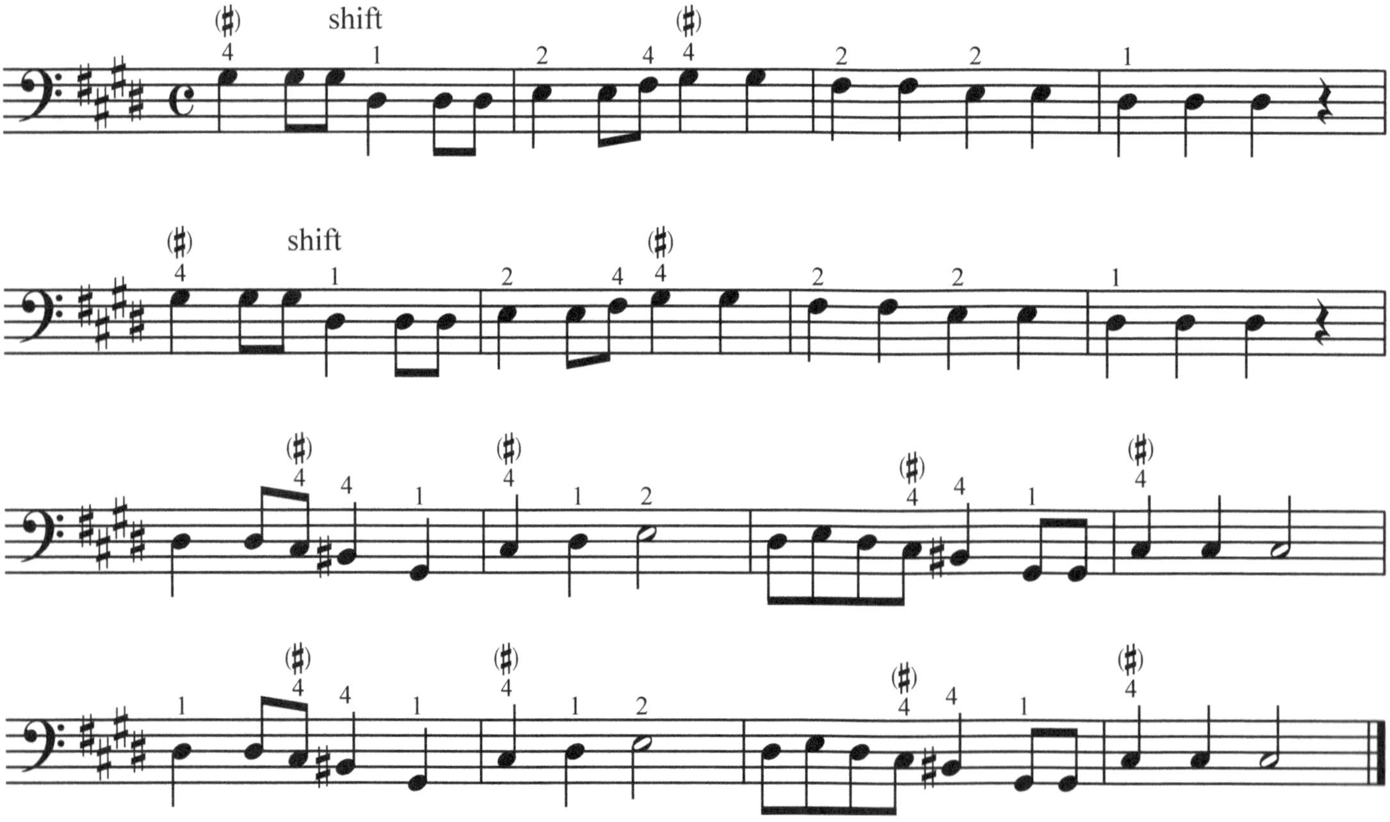

Half Position for the Cello

41

Gladioli

©2011 C. Harvey Publications All Rights Reserved.

The Bitter Wind

43

Hungarian Folk Song

Pieces for Review

Chant of the Slugs

American Summer

A Quandary

Finnish Folk Song

Finnish Folk Song

The Northern Lass: A Scottish Melody

©2011 C. Harvey Publications All Rights Reserved.

Half Position for the Cello

Good Day: A Russian Folk Song

All Through the Night: A Welsh Folk Song

©2011 C. Harvey Publications All Rights Reserved.

48

A Health to Betty: Scottish Folk Song

Half Position for the Cello

©2011 C. Harvey Publications All Rights Reserved.

Half Position Notes

Also available from www.charveypublications.com: CHP363
The Romberg Cello Sonata in E Minor Practice Edition

Preparatory Exercises for Movement One

1. Fourth Position Notes and Bowing
Measures 1-3

©2020 C. Harvey Publications   All Rights Reserved.

www.ingramcontent.com/pod-product-compliance
Lightning Source LLC
Chambersburg PA
CBHW081733100526
44591CB00016B/2601